150

First French
Phrases

Angela Wilkes

DORLING KINDERSLEY
London • New York • Stuttgart • Moscow

How to use this book

> Hi! I'm Emma.

Start speaking French today. **Emma, Eddie, Erin, and their friends** will teach you 150 simple phrases. You can say the phrases to your friends and family or try them on holiday in France. Here you can find out how to use the book.

Colour-coded contents
The book covers 12 main subjects. They are colour-coded for easy reference by tabs on the side of each page. You will find the key to the tabs on the front jacket flap.

> Hello, I'm Eddie.

Phrases
Each phrase is numbered and given in English first. A speech bubble then gives you the phrase in French.

Title
The title tells you what the page is about. It is followed by a brief introduction.

Shopping for food
Here and over the page you can learn how to ask for things and find out how much they cost.

61 Four oranges.
> Quatre oranges.

Katr' oronj.

62 A kilo of apples, please.
> Un kilo de pommes, s'il vous plaît.

Uh keelo duh pom, seel-voo-play.

63 How much is it?
> Ça fait combien?

Sa fay kawm-bee-yah?

64 Ten francs fifty.
> Dix francs cinquante.

Dee frong sankont.

20

Pronunciation guide
Beneath the picture is a pronunciation guide. It shows you how to say the French phrase. Practise reading the phrase out loud so that you know what it should sound like.

Ten useful phrases

Ten of the most useful phrases in the book are listed on the back jacket flap so that you can find them quickly.

Everyday situations

The book gives you French phrases to use in all sorts of situations. Always be polite when you are talking to people and remember to say please.

Index

If you want to find a particular word or phrase, look it up in the index. English words are listed first followed by French words.

Wordlist

Many subjects are followed by an illustrated wordlist that gives you extra vocabulary. Each word is listed in English and French and followed by a pronunciation guide. You can use words from the wordlist to vary the phrases.

Note on French nouns

As you learn French, you will notice that the word for "the" or "a" changes. This is because French nouns are masculine or feminine and the word for "the" or "a" changes accordingly.

Hello, I'm Erin.

First words

Here are some words and phrases
you will need in everyday situations.

1 Hello!

Salut!

2 Good morning.

Bonjour.

Salew!

Bawn-joor.

3 Good evening.

Bonsoir.

4 Goodbye.

Au revoir.

5 Goodnight.

Bonne nuit.

Bawn-swar.

Oh revwar.

Bon nwee.

6 Yes.
Oui.

Wee.

7 No.
Non.

Naw.

8 Please.
S'il vous plaît.

Seel-voo-play.

9 Thank you.
Merci.

Mairsee.

10 Excuse me.
Pardon.

Par-dawn.

11 Sorry.
Je m'excuse.

Juh mexkewz.

Helpful phrases

Here are some more phrases that you will find useful when you start to speak French.

12 How are things?

Ça va?

Sa va?

13 Fine, thanks.

Ça va bien, merci.

Sa va beeyah, mairsee.

14 See you soon.

À bientôt.

A beeyah-toh.

15 Do you speak English?

Parlez-vous anglais?

Parlay vooz onglay?

16 A little.

Un peu.

Uh puh.

17 I don't speak French.

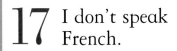

> Je ne parle pas français.

Juh nuh parl pa fronsay.

18 More slowly, please.

> Plus lentement, s'il vous plaît.

Plew lontuhmon, seel-voo-play.

19 I don't understand.

> Je ne comprends pas.

Juh nuh compron pa.

20 Can you repeat that, please?

> Encore une fois, s'il vous plaît.

Onkor ewn fwa, seel-voo-play.

Finding the way

Here and over the page you can find out
how to ask for simple directions.

21 Excuse me, where's the Café Flora?

Pardon, où se trouve le Café Flora?

Par-dawn, oo suh troov luh kaffay Flora?

22 It's over there ...

C'est là-bas ...

Say la ba ...

23 ... opposite the cathedral.

... en face de la cathédrale.

... on fass duh la kataydral.

24 Where are the shops?

Où se trouvent les magasins?

Oo suh troov lay magaza?

25 They are in Church Street.

Ils sont rue de l'Église.

Eel son rew duh laygleez.

26 Is it far?

C'est loin?

Say lwa?

27 About five minutes on foot.

Cinq minutes à pied, environ.

Sank meenoot a pee-yay, onveeron.

28 Is there a supermarket near here?

Est-ce qu'il y a un supermarché près d'ici?

Esk-eel-ya uh sewpermarshay pray-dee-see?

29 Yes, just next to the bank.

Oui, juste à côté de la banque.

Wee, jewst a kohtay duh la bonk.

9

30 Excuse me, how do I get to the station?

31 Take the first street on the right ...

Pardon, pour aller à la gare?

Vous prenez la première rue à droite ...

Par-dawn, poor allay a la gar?

Voo prenay la premyair rew a drwat ...

32 ... then the second street on the left ...

33 ... and go straight on as far as the station.

... puis la deuxième rue à gauche ...

... et continuez tout droit jusqu' à la gare.

... pwee la duhzyem rew a gohsh ...

... ay kon-tin-yew-ay too drwa jewska la gar.

Wordlist

information
informations
an-for-ma-see-yon

hotel
hôtel
ohtel

campsite
camping
kompeeng

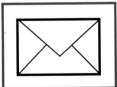

city centre
centre-ville
sontr veel

post office
la poste
la posst

market
marché
marshay

chemist
pharmacie
farmasee

telephone
téléphone
taylayfon

toilets
toilettes
twalet

bus stop
arrêt de bus
array duh bews

airport
aéroport
ayropor

traffic lights
feux
fuh

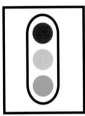

bridge
pont
pon

crossroads
carrefour
karfoor

bend
virage
veeraj

At the café

To order something, just name it and say "please".
You also say "please" to call over the waitress.

34 Please!

S'il vous plaît!

Seel-voo-play!

35 What would you like?

Vous désirez?

Voo dayzeeray?

36 A coffee, please.

Un café, s'il vous plaît.

Uh kaffay, seel-voo-play.

37 And an apple juice for me.

Et pour moi un jus de pommes.

Ay poor mwa uh jew duh pom.

38 Right away.

Tout-de-suite.

Toot sweet.

39 Do you have sandwiches?

Vous avez des sandwichs?

Voos avay day sondweesh?

40 Yes – ham and cheese.

Oui – jambon et fromage.

Wee – jombon ay fromaj.

41 A ham sandwich, please.

Un sandwich au jambon, s'il vous plaît.

Uh sondweesh oh jombon, seel-voo-play.

42 Fine.

Très bien.

Tray beeyah.

13

43 What kinds of ice-cream do you have?

Qu'est-ce que vous avez comme glaces?

Keskuh vooz avay kom glas?

44 Vanilla, strawberry, and chocolate.

Vanille, fraise, et chocolat.

Vanee, frez, ay shokolah.

45 A vanilla ice-cream, please.

Une glace à la vanille, s'il vous plaît.

Ewn glas a la vanee, seel-voo-play.

46 And a lolly for me.

Et un esquimau pour moi.

Ay uhn eskeemoh poor mwa.

47 How much is that?

Ça fait combien?

Sa fay kawm-bee-yah?

48 Eight francs, please.

Huit francs, s'il vous plaît.

Wee frong, seel-voo-play.

Wordlist

an orange juice
un jus d'orange
uh jew doranj

a mineral water
une eau minérale
ewn oh meenayral

a lemonade
une limonade
ewn leemohnahd

with ice
avec des glaçons
avek day glasson

a milkshake
un milkshake
uh meelkshek

a cup of ...
une tasse de ...
ewn tass duh ...

a tea with milk
un thé au lait
uh tay oh lay

a hot chocolate
un chocolat chaud
uh shokolah show

some sugar
du sucre
dew sewkr

a pizza
une pizza
ewn pizza

a hamburger
un hamburger
uhn awm-boor-gair

a toasted sandwich
un croque-monsieur
uh krok muhsyuh

some crisps
des chips
day sheeps

a cake
un gâteau
uh gahtoh

At the restaurant

We say "I'll have…" to order food. French people say "Je prends…", which means "I'll take …".

49 A table for two, please.

> Une table pour deux personnes, s'il vous plaît.

Ewn tabl poor duh pairson, seel-voo-play.

50 The menu, please.

> La carte, s'il vous plaît.

La kart, seel-voo-play.

51 Have you chosen?

> Vous avez choisi?

52 I'll have steak and chips.

> Je prends un steak-frites.

Vooz avay shwazee?

Juh pron uh stayk-freet.

53 For the main course, I'll have a pork chop.

Comme plat principal, je prends une côte de porc.

Kom plah pranseepal, juh pron ewn kot duh por.

54 And for dessert, an apple tart.

Et comme dessert, une tarte aux pommes.

Ay kom desair, ewn tart oh pom.

55 And to drink?

Et comme boisson?

Ay kom bwasson?

56 What's this please?

Qu'est-ce que c'est, s'il vous plaît?

Keskuh say, seel-voo-play?

57 More bread, please.

Encore du pain, s'il vous plaît.

Onkor dew pa, seel-voo-play.

58 Have you finished?

Vous avez terminé?

Vooz avay tair-mee-nay?

59 The bill, please.

L'addition, s'il vous plaît.

Ladeesyon, seel-voo-play.

60 Is service included?

Est-ce que le service est compris?

Eskuh luh sairvees ay kawmpree?

Wordlist

soup
le potage
luh potaj

fish
le poisson
luh pwasson

meat
la viande
la veeyond

chicken
le poulet
luh poolay

vegetables
les légumes
lay laygewm

salad
la salade
la salad

pasta
les pâtes
lay pat

rice
le riz
luh ree

fruit
les fruits
lay frwee

pudding
le dessert
luh dessair

salt
le sel
luh sel

pepper
le poivre
luh pwahvr

a knife
un couteau
uh kootoh

a fork
une fourchette
ewn foorshet

a spoon
une cuillère
ewn kwee-yair

19

Shopping for food

Here and over the page you can learn how to ask for things and find out how much they cost.

61 Four oranges.

Quatre oranges.

62 A kilo of apples, please.

Un kilo de pommes, s'il vous plaît.

Katr' oronj.

Uh keelo duh pom, seel-voo-play.

63 How much is it?

Ça fait combien?

Sa fay kawm-bee-yah?

64 Ten francs fifty.

Dix francs cinquante.

Dee frong sankont.

65 How much are the tomatoes?

66 Eight francs a kilo.

C'est combien, les tomates?

Huit francs le kilo.

Say kawm-bee-yah, lay tomaht?

Wee frong luh keelo.

67 Have you got a bag, please?

68 Of course. There you are.

Vous avez un sac, s'il vous plaît?

Bien sûr. Voilà!

Vooz avay uh sak, seel-voo-play?

Beeyah sewr. Vwa-lah!

69 A piece of that cheese, please.

Un morceau de ce fromage là, s'il vous plaît.

Uh morsoh duh suh fromaj la, seel-voo-play.

70 This much?

Comme ceci?

Kom suh-see?

71 A bit more.

Encore un peu.

Onkor uh puh.

72 That's fine.

Ça ira.

Sa eera.

73 Anything else?

Avec ceci?

Avek suh-see?

74 That's all. How much is it?

C'est tout. Ça fait combien?

Say too. Sa fay kawm-bee-yah?

Wordlist

a loaf of bread
un pain
uh pa

bread rolls
des petits pains
day puhtee pa

butter
du beurre
dew bur

half a litre of milk
un demi-litre de lait
*uh duhmee leetre
duh lay*

eggs
des œufs
dayz uh

a jar of jam
un pot de confiture
*uh poh duh
kon-fee-tewr*

biscuits
des biscuits
day beeskwee

strawberries
des fraises
day frez

bananas
des bananes
day banan

grapes
des raisins
day rayza

potatoes
des pommes de terre
day pom duh tair

a bottle of …
une bouteille de …
ewn bootay duh …

a tin of …
une boîte de …
ewn bwat duh …

a packet of …
une boîte de …
ewn bwat duh …

Shopping for clothes

These phrases are useful when you are shopping for clothes.

75 Can I help you?

> Je peux vous aider?

Juh puh vooz ayday?

76 I'm just looking, thank you.

> Je regarde seulement, merci.

Juh ruhgard suhlmon, mairsee.

77 Do you have this jumper in blue?

> Avez-vous ce pull en bleu?

Avay voo suh pewl on bluh?

78 Yes. In blue, red, and yellow.

> Oui. En bleu, en rouge, et en jaune.

Wee. On bluh, on rooj, ay on joan.

79

Can I try it on?

Je peux l'essayer?

Juh puh lessay-ay?

80

Go ahead!

Allez-y!

Allay-zee!

81

I'll take this one.

Je vais prendre celui-ci.

82

That's 160 francs.

Ça fait cent soixante francs.

Juh vay prondr suhlwee-see.

Sa fay son swasont frong.

Wordlist

T-shirt
le tee-shirt
luh tee-shert

shorts
le short
luh short

skirt
la jupe
la jewp

trousers
le pantalon
luh pontalon

sweatshirt
le sweat-shirt
luh swet-shert

dress
la robe
la rob

shoes
les chaussures
lay shohsewr

swimsuit
le maillot de bain
luh myoh duh ba

trainers
les baskets
lay bask-et

cap
la casquette
la kask-et

sunglasses
les lunettes de soleil
lay lewnet duh solay

bag
le sac
luh sak

watch
la montre
la montr

comb
le peigne
luh peng

brush
la brosse
la bross

soap
le savon
luh savon

toothpaste
le dentifrice
luh don-tee-frees

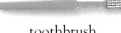

toothbrush
la brosse à dents
la bross a don

plasters
les sparadraps
lay spa-ra-drah

postcard
la carte postale
la kart postahl

pencil
le crayon
luh krayon

pen
le stylo
luh steelo

crayons
les crayons de couleur
lay krayon duh kooluhr

envelopes
les enveloppes
layz on-vuh-lop

paper
le papier
luh pap-ee-yay

camera
l'appareil-photo
laparay foto

film
la pellicule
la peli-kewl

book
le livre
luh leevr

ball
le ballon
luh ballon

goggles
les lunettes de plongée
lay lewnet duh plonjay

boat
le bateau
luh batoh

car
la voiture
la vwatewr

doll
la poupée
la poopay

Post offices and banks

Here you can find out how to ask for
things in a post office or bank.

83 How much is a
stamp for England?

C'est
combien, un
timbre pour
l'Angleterre?

*Say kawm-bee-yah, uh
tambr poor longluhtair?*

84 It's for a postcard.

C'est
pour
une
carte
postale.

*Say poor ewn
kart postahl.*

85 I'd like to send this letter
to New York.

Je voudrais
envoyer
cette lettre à
New York.

*Juh voodrayz on-vwi-
yay set letr a noo york.*

86 I'd like to change some pounds sterling.

Je voudrais changer des livres sterling.

Juh voodray shonjay day leevr stairleeng.

87 How much do you want to change?

Combien voulez-vous changer?

Kawm-bee-yah voolay voo shonjay?

88 Twenty pounds, please.

Vingt livres sterling, s'il vous plait.

Va leevr stairleeng, seel-voo-play.

Wordlist

a post-box
une boîte à lettres
ewn bwat a letr

traveller's cheques
des chèques de voyage
day shek duh vwa-yaj

a parcel
un paquet
uh pakay

by airmail
par avion
par aveeyon

Sightseeing

Use these phrases to ask for information at a tourist office and places you visit.

89 Do you have a street map?

> **Vous avez un plan de la ville?**

Vooz avay uh plon duh la veel?

90 Can you show me on the map?

> **Vous pouvez me le montrer sur le plan?**

Voo poovay muh luh montray sewr luh plon?

91 When is the museum open?

> **Quelles sont les heures d'ouverture du musée?**

Kell son layz uhr doo-vair-tewr dew mewzay?

92 Every day, except Tuesdays.

> **Tous les jours, sauf le mardi.**

Too lay joor, sohf luh mardee.

93
How much is it to get in?

C'est combien, le billet d'entrée?

Say kawm-bee-yah, luh bee-yay dontray?

94
Two adults and a child, please.

Deux adultes et un enfant, s'il vous plaît.

Duhz adewlt ay uhn onfon, seel-voo-play.

95
I'd like a guide book please.

Je voudrais un guide, s'il vous plaît.

Juh voodrayz uh geed, seel-voo-play.

96
Can I take photos?

On peut prendre des photos?

Awn puh prondr day fohtoh?

97
Are there guided tours?

Est-ce qu'il y a des visites guidées?

Esk-eel-ya day veezeet geeday?

98
When does the tour begin?

La visite guidée commence à quelle heure?

La veezeet geeday komons a kel uhr?

Wordlist

zoo
le zoo
luh zoh

funfair
la fête foraine
la fet foren

playground
le terrain de jeux
luh teran duh juh

boat trip
la promenade en bateau
la promnad on batoh

sports ground
le terrain de sport
luh teran duh spor

circus
le cirque
luh seerk

cinema
le cinéma
luh seenayma

theatre
le théâtre
luh tay-atr

art gallery
le musée d'art
luh mewzay dar

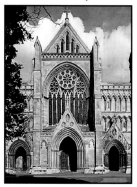

church
l'église
laygleez

lake
le lac
luh lak

seaside
le bord de la mer
luh bor duh la mair

mountains
les montagnes
lay montan

harbour
le port
luh por

farm
la ferme
la fairm

Danger!
Danger!
Donjay!

No swimming.
Baignade interdite.
Bayn-yahd anterdeet.

Beware of the dog.
Chien méchant.
Sheeya mayshon.

Do not touch.
Défense de toucher.
Dayfons duh tooshay.

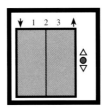

lift
ascenseur
asonsuhr

stairs
escalier
eskalyay

tickets
billets
bee-yay

Open
Ouvert
Oovair

Shut
Fermé
Fairmay

Way out/Exit
Sortie
Sortee

You are here.
Vous êtes ici.
Vooz et eesee.

Entrance
Entrée
Ontray

Emergency exit
Sortie de secours
Sortee duh skoor

No entry.
Entrée interdite.
Ontray anterdeet.

Opening hours
Heures d'ouverture
Uhr doo-vair-tewr

Admission free
Entrée gratuite
Ontray gratweet

Cash desk
Caisse
Kes

At the hotel

These phrases will help you to ask for information at a hotel and book a room.

99 Do you have a room?

> Est-ce que vous avez une chambre?

Eskuh vooz avay ewn shombr?

100 For how many people?

> Pour combien de personnes?

Poor kawm-bee-yah duh pairson?

101 For two adults and one child.

> Pour deux adultes et un enfant.

Poor duhz adewlt ay uhn onfon.

102 A room with a bathroom?

> Une chambre avec salle de bains?

Ewn shombr avek sal duh ban?

103 How many nights are you staying?

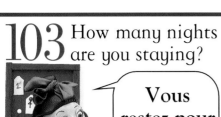

Vous restez pour combien de nuits?

Voo restay poor kawm-bee-yah duh nwee?

104 For two nights.

Pour deux nuits.

Poor duh nwee.

105 Is breakfast included?

Le petit déjeuner est compris?

Luh puhtee day-juh-nay ay kawmpree?

106 It's room number five.

C'est la chambre numéro cinq.

Say la shombr new-mayro sank.

107 Here's your key.

Voici votre clé.

Vwasee votr klay.

Making friends

Use these phrases to tell new friends something about yourself.

108 What's your name?

Comment tu t'appelles?

Komon tew tapel?

109 My name is Emma.

Je m'appelle Emma.

Juh mapel Emma.

110 How old are you?

Quel âge as-tu?

Kel aj a tew?

111 I am eight.

J'ai huit ans.

Jay weet on.

112 Where are you from?

Tu viens d'où?

Tew veean doo?

113 I'm from London.

Je suis de Londres.

Juh swee duh londr.

114 Are you on holiday?

Tu es en vacances?

Tew ayz on vakons?

115 Yes, with my family.

Oui, avec ma famille.

Wee, avek ma fa-mee.

116 Do you have any brothers and sisters?

Tu as des frères et des sœurs?

Tew a day frair ay day suhr?

117 I have one brother.

J'ai un frère.

Jay uh frair.

At the station

You will need these phrases if you buy tickets or ask for information at a railway station.

118 A ticket for Paris, please.

Un billet pour Paris, s'il vous plaît.

Uh bee-yay poor paree, seel-voo-play.

119 Single or return?

Aller-simple ou aller-retour?

Allay sampl oo allay ruhtoor?

120 A return ticket.

Un billet aller-retour.

Uh bee-yay allay ruhtoor.

121 A timetable, please.

Les horaires, s'il vous plaît.

Layz or-air, seel-voo-play.

122 What time is the next train to Paris?

Le prochain train pour Paris part à quelle heure?

Luh prosha tra poor paree par a kel uhr?

123 Which platform does the Paris train leave from?

Le train pour Paris part de quel quai?

Luh tra poor paree par duh kel kay?

124 From platform four.

Du quai numéro quatre.

Dew kay new-mayro katr.

125 Is this the Paris train?

C'est bien le train pour Paris?

Say beeyah luh tra poor paree?

126 Yes. You have to change at Lyon.

Oui. Il faut changer à Lyon.

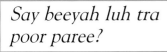

Wee. Il foh shonjay a leeyon.

Telling the time

Here you can find out how to ask and tell the time. Turn the page to learn more numbers.

127 What time is it?

Quelle heure est-il?

128 It's one o'clock.

Il est une heure.

Kel uhr ay teel?

Eel et ewn uhr.

129

two o'clock
deux heures
duhz uhr

130

five past two
deux heures cinq
duhz uhr sank

131

quarter past two
deux heures et quart
duhz uhr ay kar

132

half past two
deux heures et demie
duz uhr ay duhmee

133

quarter to three
trois heures moins le quart
trwaz uhr mwa luh kar

134

five to three
trois heures moins cinq
trwaz uhr mwa sank

135

in the morning
du matin
dew mata

136

in the afternoon
de l'après-midi
duh lapray meedee

137

in the evening
du soir
dew swar

138

at midday
à midi
a meedee

139

at midnight
à minuit
a meenwee

140

in half an hour
dans une demi-heure
donz ewn duhmee uhr

Numbers

1
un
uh

2
deux
duh

3
trois
trwa

4
quatre
katr

5
cinq
sank

6
six
sees

7
sept
set

8
huit
weet

9
neuf
nuhf

10
dix
dees

11
onze
awnz

12
douze
dooz

13
treize
trez

14
quatorze
katorz

15
quinze
kanz

16
seize
sez

17
dix-sept
deeset

18
dix-huit
deezweet

19
dix-neuf
deeznuhf

20
vingt
va

21
vingt et un
vantay uh

22
vingt-deux
van duh

23
vingt-trois
van trwa

24
vingt-quatre
van katr

25
vingt-cinq
van sank

26
vingt-six
van sees

27
vingt-sept
van set

28
vingt-huit
vant weet

29
vingt-neuf
van nuhf

30
trente
tront

40
quarante
karont

50
cinquante
sankont

60
soixante
swasont

70
soixante-dix
swasont dees

80
quatre-vingts
katr va

90
quatre-vingt-dix
katr van dees

100
cent
son

Colours

red
rouge
rooj

yellow
jaune
joan

blue
bleu
bluh

green
vert
vair

purple
violet
veeyolay

orange
orange
oranj

brown
marron
maron

white
blanc
blon

black
noir
nwar

Days

Monday
lundi
luhdee

Tuesday
mardi
mardee

Wednesday
mercredi
maircruhdee

Thursday
jeudi
juhdee

Friday
vendredi
vondruhdee

Saturday
samedi
samdee

Sunday
dimanche
deemonsh

week
la semaine
la suhmen

weekend
le week-end
luh weekend

Help!

These phrases are useful when you need help, have hurt yourself, or feel ill.

141 Can you help me?

> **Pourriez-vous m'aider?**

Pooreeay voo mayday?

142 I'm lost.

> **Je suis perdue.**

Juh swee pairdew.

143 I've lost my passport.

> **J'ai perdu mon passeport.**

Jay pairdew mon paspor.

144 My wallet has been stolen.

> **On m'a volé mon portefeuille.**

On ma volay mon port-fuh-yee.

145 My camera isn't working.

Mon appareil-photo ne marche pas.

Mon aparay foto nuh marsh pa.

146 Help!

Au secours!

Oh skoor!

147 There's been an accident.

Il y a eu un accident.

Eel-ya ew uhn ak-seedon.

148 I've cut myself.

Je me suis coupé.

Juh muh swee koopay.

149 I don't feel well.

Je ne me sens pas bien.

Juh nuh muh son pa beeyah.

150 Where does it hurt?

Où avez-vous mal?

Oo avay voo mal?

English index

In each index, only one page reference is given for each word or phrase, unless a word or phrase has more than one translation.

French index

Note: In this index nouns are preceded by the French words for "the". "Le" precedes masculine nouns, "la" feminine nouns, "les" plural nouns, and "l' " nouns beginning with a vowel.